Welcome to
MEXICO

Text by Margaret Friskey
Sketches by Lois Axeman

 CHILDRENS PRESS, CHICAGO

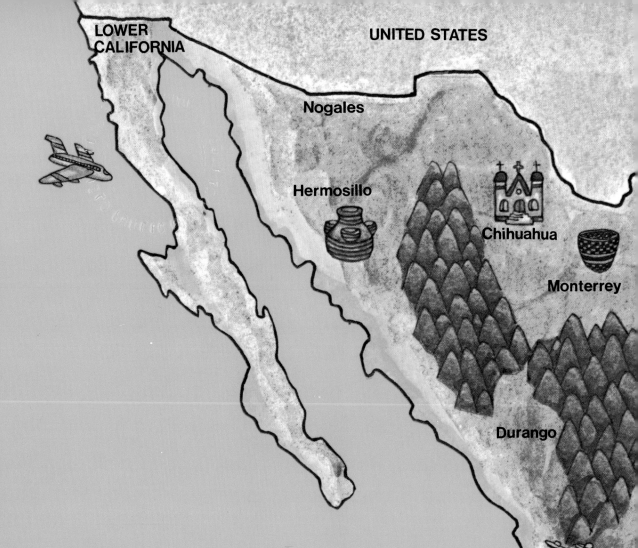

LOWER CALIFORNIA

UNITED STATES

Nogales

Hermosillo

Chihuahua

Monterrey

Durango

Guadalajara
㊴ ㊶ ㊸ ㊺

PACIFIC OCEAN

Welcome to the World Books
Created by T. A. Chacharon & Associates, Ltd.

Library of Congress Cataloging in Publication Data
Friskey, Margaret, 1901-
    Welcome to Mexico.
    (Welcome to the world)
    SUMMARY: Simple text and illustrations introduce
    the tourist attractions of Mexico.
1. Mexico—Description and travel—1951-
—Juvenile literature. [1. Mexico—Description and travel]
I. Axeman Lois, ill. II. Title.
F1208.5.F74   917.2'04'82   74-28160
ISBN 0-516-03712-9

Photographs courtesy of Mexican National Tourist Bureau.

UNITED STATES

N

W E

S

GULF OF MEXICO

scale of miles

0   100   200

Zacatecas

Guanajuato ㉑

Patzcuaro ⑲

Mexico City ⑮ ⑰
④ ⑦ ⑨ ⑪ ⑬

Cuernavaca

Taxco
㉓ ㉕ ㉗

Oaxaca
㉙ ㉛ ㉝ ㉟
㊲

Acapulco

YUCATAN

CAMPECHE

GUATAMALA

3

Welcome to Mexico City. The big, noisy,
colorful capital of Mexico.

It is the oldest city in North America.
So old that no one knows for sure where
the first people came from.

It is also as new as a gleaming skyscraper
and a broad, beautiful boulevard.

The main streets have many circles called
glorietas. Traffic is heavy.

Take a walk in the bright sunshine and
clear air of this unusual city.

Do not hurry. You might have to stop and
catch your breath.

Mexico City is a mile and a half high.
It lies on a plateau where two mountain
ranges meet. They say it is floating on
an old lake bed.

Start in the Old City. This was once a little island a quarter of a mile across.

Temples, pyramids, and palaces of the Aztec Indians were built here.

The Aztecs came in 1325, and they were not the first. Other Indians had been building civilizations in Mexico for two thousand years.

The Toltecs had built a city near here. But they had moved on by the time the Aztecs came.

Hernan Cortez captured the Aztecs. The Spanish ruled Mexico for three hundred years.

Now Mexico is a republic. The president serves for six years.

This is the Plaza of Three Cultures. There are Aztec ruins, a church built by the Spaniards, and modern government buildings.

There were over sixty thousand families here when the Dutch were settling on Manhattan Island.

Stop at the Alameda. This park was
once the Aztec market place. It was joined
to the old city by a causeway.

The cruel Spaniards burned non-believers
at the stake here.

Now it is a big, beautiful park.

You cannot miss the large marble statue
of Benito Juarez, an Indian. He was president
of Mexico, and considered its greatest hero.

Chapultepec Park in the heart of the city was the Aztec hunting ground. It is so big that it never seems crowded.

There are woods and lakes. There is a zoo and an amusement park.

There are many museums. Do not miss the famous and beautiful Museum of Anthropology.

You can see a model of the Aztec capital, the giant stone heads, and other treasures from earlier civilizations in Mexico.

Monolitos Fountain is in the new Chapultepec Park.

Ride a barge in Xochimilco Park. These islands are called the floating gardens.

When the Aztecs lived here, the whole valley was a lake. They built rafts, covered them with dirt, and planted gardens. As years went by, the rafts took root. They are not floating any more. Many vegetables and flowers for the city are grown here. And a ride through the canals is delightful.

Mexican families come on Sunday. They have a picnic on a flower-trimmed boat and listen to the bands play.

Travel just a few miles from Mexico City into the dim past of the country.

The enormous Pyramid of the Sun, and the smaller Pyramid of the Moon, stand guard over the ruins of an ancient city.

This city was old and in ruins by the time the Aztecs settled on their island.

It is believed that this was the holy city of the Toltec Indians.

The huge pyramids dominate the Street of the Dead. It is an eerie place.

Come here, any night except Monday, at seven o'clock, from October through May. A Light and Sound show is given in English at that time. It dramatizes the story of these early people and their civilization.

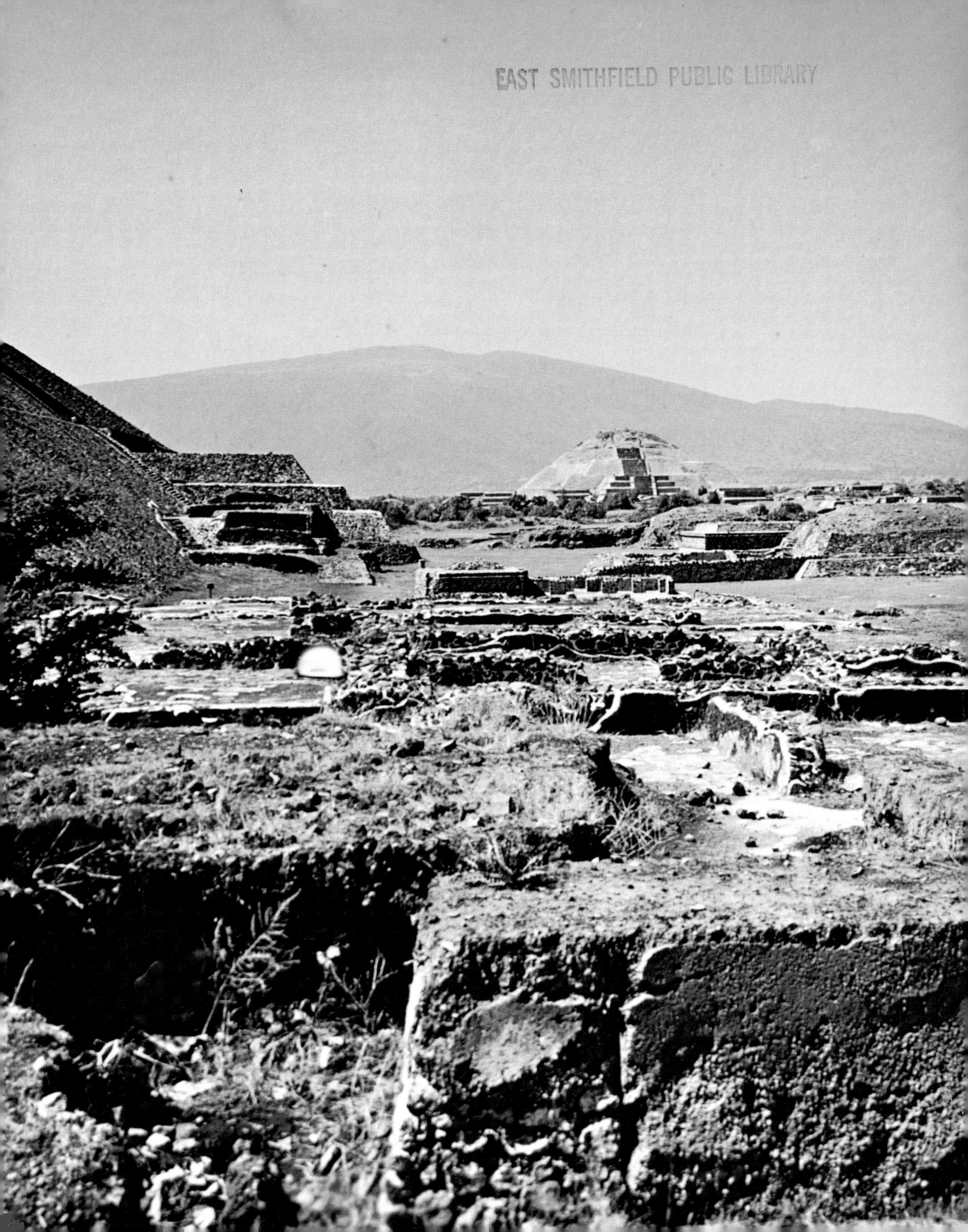

Mexico has many kinds of climate.

Cuernavaca is two thousand feet lower than Mexico City. It is a little warmer. People come here to get away from the winter chill in Mexico City.

Cortez built a palace here in 1530. It is now a museum with some fine murals by Rivera.

Another delightful week-end retreat from the city is Patzcuaro. A quiet town in the Tarascan Indian country. It is famous for its fishermen who go out with their huge butterfly nets.

On Wednesdays you can see the Dance of the Old Men. Friday mornings the plaza comes alive with the Indian market.

Step back into Spanish colonial days in the charming town of Guanajuato. It nestles in a canyon between two mountains.

Walk its narrow, cobbled, twisting streets. The Spaniards found the richest silver mines in the world here. They settled down, mined the silver, and sent it to Spain.

You can go down into the ruins of an old silver mine. Then listen to a band concert on the plaza.

Take a scary walk through the halls of the Pantheon. They are lined with mummies.

Enjoy the beautiful Castle of Santa Cecilia. It is really a hotel.

Taxco is a Spanish colonial city, too.
It is so unusual that it has been made a
national monument.

Silver built the city.

They tell a story about the Spaniard who
found the rich silver lode here.

He was riding through these mountains
when his horse got stuck in the mud. When
he pulled his foot out, there was the silver.

The Spanish silver baron was so grateful
for this good luck that he built a church
that dominates the town.

It was a boom town while the silver lasted.
Then, for a while, it was almost a ghost town.

About fifty years ago, an American found
Taxco. He liked it so much he settled there.
He began designing and making silver jewelry.
Now, many craftsmen working with silver have
brought the town to life.

There are several hundred silver shops.

Walk the steep, cobbled streets of Taxco, with its whitewashed houses and its red tile roofs.

Indians come to town on Sundays and set up their market.

There is an annual silver fair in Taxco early in December.

Buy a piñata and have a Mexican party.

A piñata is a clay pot full of candy and fruit covered by a paper figure. You put on blindfolds and try to break the pot with a stick.

Oaxaca is a favorite city to visit. It is 340 miles southeast of Mexico City. It is in a valley surrounded by mountains.

The Spanish built many buildings here. They tried to make this a Spanish city. One unusual church has walls thirty feet thick.

But Oaxaca has remained an Indian city.

Indian ruins on a plateau overlooking the city date back to 500 B.C. Digging is still being done here.

The State Museum in Oaxaca has hundreds of pieces of jade, silver, gold, and turquoise that were found in one tomb.

Oaxaca is very gay. There is music every day in the square.

Twice a week a sixty-piece band plays.

Other times there are small groups.

There are many fiestas here. The biggest one is held in July near the statue of Juarez. He came from here.

There are harvest festivals. Then, as Christmas approaches, there are dances, parades, and parties every day.

A special radish-carving contest is held on the night of December 23.

Dances and costumes make Oaxaca colorful.

People dance on holy days. They dance to celebrate the harvest. They dance to honor heroes.

Children like to stay out of school on fiesta days.

All Mexican children are supposed to go through the primary grades at least.

This is hard for some of them. There are still fifty Indian languages spoken in Mexico.

Oaxaca is a center for crafts. Green
earthenware and Oaxaca black pottery
are famous.
    No two pieces are exactly alike.
    Each one is made by hand.

Saturday is market day in Oaxaca.

Indians come from all the surrounding villages. Many of them walk a long way with their heavy loads.

They bring hand-woven fabrics, straw baskets and hats, clay figures, leather goods, jewelry, pottery, and food from their gardens.

You can buy almost anything here from a little clay pig to a hand-tooled saddle.

You could go southwest from Mexico
City to Acapulco. It is on the Pacific
Ocean, one of the most beautiful and
modern resorts in the world.

But if you go northwest, you will
come to Guadalajara. This is the second
largest city in Mexico. It has kept its
old Spanish charm.

There are many small farms in this
area. It is the bread-basket of Mexico.

Ride a carriage to see this beautiful,
flower-filled city.

Ride the Toonerville train around the Parque Agua Azul.

There is an open-air theater here, and a bird sanctuary.

Guadalajara is a city of parks.

In Alcalde Park you can whiz around the lake in a water scooter.

In another park there is a little steamer to take you around the lake.

Five miles from the center of
Guadalajara you will find a corner
of old Mexico. It was once a separate
village called Tlaquepaque.

The Mariachis came from here. These
are the bands seen all over Mexico. The
men dress like Mexican cowboys and play
guitars and trumpets.

There are glassblowers here. You can watch them work. They put on a dramatic show.

You can watch potters at work, and weavers.

This is a good place to shop. Take home a few things that will remind you of this trip.

Remember the beauty of the country, the warmth of the sun, the fun of the music, and the pride of the friendly people.

Hasta la vista

Things to do in and around Mexico City

Ride the rubber-tired subway. Pause at the Pino Suarez station to see the pyramid that the diggers found and left there.

Go to a folklore ballet.

Ride a boat in Xochimilco Park.

See Diego Rivera's murals in the central stairway of the National Palace.

From the National Palace, walk down Francisco Madero. This street leads to the Church of San Francisco. It was begun a hundred years before the Pilgrims landed at Plymouth. See the House of Tiles across the street.

Walk down elegant Juarez Avenue. Stop at Alameda Park in the heart of the city.

Read the inscription on the equestrian statue where Juarez Avenue crosses Reforma. It is an enormous statue of the Spanish king, Charles IV. The inscription says something like this: "We keep this because it is a beautiful piece of art, not because of love for Spanish royalty."

The Reforma leads to Chapultepec Park. Visit the castle. It is now the National Museum.

Spend a lot of time in the Museum of Anthropology.

Stop at the zoo and the amusement park.

Have a picnic in the National Park called Desert of the Lions, an hour's drive from the city.

Walk through the campus of the University of Mexico.

Visit the famous shrine of Our Lady of Guadalupe.

See a Mexican rodeo some Sunday morning.

Sit on the revolving platform to see the light-and-sound show at the enormous "March of Humanity" mural in the Polyforum Cultural Siqueiros.

Go to see the biggest bullring in the world. It is down in a hollow. When you walk in from the street, you are at the top of the stadium. Bullfights are held on Sunday afternoons.

Learn a few words and phrases in Spanish

Hello	Hola
Good day	Buenos días
Good night	Buenas noches
Good friends	Buenos amigos
Yes	Sí
No	No
Please	Por favor
Excuse me	Dispénseme
Wait here	Aguarda aquí
Thank you	Gracias
You're welcome	de nada
I'm sorry	lo siento mucho
Entrance	Entrada
Exit	Salida
I want	Necesito
Postcard	Tarteja postal
Stamp	Estampilla
Museum	el museo
Let's go to the park	Vamos al parque
A rest, nap	Siesta
Goodby	Adios
Until we meet again	Hasta la vista